THIS BOOK
BELONGS TO

KINGFISHER

SAINTS and ANGELS

Claire Llewellyn

KINGFISHER

KINGFISHER

Kingfisher Publications Plc
New Penderel House,
283–288 High Holborn,
London WC1V 7HZ
www.kingfisherpub.com

First published by Kingfisher Publications Plc 2003
2 4 6 8 10 9 7 5 3 1
1TR/0503/SF/MAR(MAR)/150ENSOMA

A CIP catalogue record for this book is available from the British Library.

ISBN 0 7534 0812 0

Consultant: Annette Reynolds at AD Publishing Services
Editor: Carron Brown
Senior designer: Jane Tassie
Picture researcher: Rachael Swann
DTP coordinator: Sarah Pfitzner
Artwork archivists: Wendy Allison, Steve Robinson
Production controller: Debbie Otter
Indexer: Chris Bernstein

Printed in China

Acknowledgements

The publishers would like to thank the following for supplying photographs for this book:
b = bottom, *c* = centre, *l* = left, *t* = top, *m* = middle, *r* = right

cover and presentation page: The National Gallery, London; pages: 1 The Bridgeman Art Library, London; 3 *tr* AKG London/S. Domingie; 4 *tl* AKG London/Cameraphoto; 4 *br* Scala; 5 *t* The National Gallery, London; 6 The National Gallery, London; 7 *tr* Scala; 8 *bl* AKG London; 9 *tl* Scala; 10 *tl* AKG London/Cameraphoto; 11 AKG London/Erich Lessing; 12 The National Gallery, London; 13 *tr* Scala; 15 The Art Archive/Fine Art Museum, Bilbao/Dagli Orti (A); 16 Scala; 17 *br* The Art Archive/Dagli Orti; 18 *bl* The National Gallery, London; 19 *br* The National Gallery, London; 20 *bl* The Art Archive/Biblioteca Nazionale Marciana, Venice/Dagli Orti (A); 21 *tl* AKG London/Cameraphoto; 22 *cr* AKG London/S. Domingie; 23 *br* Scala; 24 The Bridgeman Art Library/Galleria Borghese, Rome, Italy; 26 *bl* The National Gallery, London; 27 The Art Archive/Accademia Carrara, Bergamo, Italy/Dagli Orti; 28 *bl* The National Gallery, London; 29 *r* The National Gallery, London; 30 *bl* AKG London; 31 *tr* AKG Berlin/S.Domingie; 32 Bridgeman Giraudon/Lauros; 33 *tr* The Art Archive/MusZe Thomas DobZe, Nantes/Dagli Orti; 34 *cl* AKG London/Cameraphoto; 35 Scala; 36 AKG London/Cameraphoto; 37 *tr* The Bridgeman Art Library, London/Huntington Library and Art Gallery, San Marino, CA, USA; 38 *bl* Scala; 39 *tl* The Bridgeman Art Library, London/Fitzwilliam Museum, University of Cambridge, UK; 40 *bl* AKG London/Erich Lessing; 41 The Art Archive; 43 *bl* The Bridgeman Art Library, London; 43 *br* AKG London/Cameraphoto; 44 *bl* The Bridgeman Art Library, London/Galleria Nazionale dell'Umbria, Perugia, Italy; 45 *br* The Bridgeman Art Library, London/Archives Charmet; 48 *bl* Scala; 49 *tr* AKG London/Erich Lessing; 50 *tl* The Bridgeman Art Library/Cameraphoto Arte Venezia: 51 *bl* AKG London/Orsi Battaglini; 52 The National Gallery, London; 53 *tr* AKG London/Erich Lessing; 54 *tl* The National Gallery, London; 54 *bm* The National Gallery, London; 55 The National Gallery, London; 56 The National Gallery, London; 57 *tr* AKG London; 58 *tl* AKG London/Gilles Mermet; 59 AKG London/Erich Lessing; 60 *tl* The Bridgeman Art Library, London/Huntington Library and Art Gallery, San Marino, CA, USA; 60 *tr* AKG London; 60 *bl* The Art Archive; 61 *tr* AKG London/Erich Lessing; 61 *cl* AKG London/Cameraphoto; 61 *br* Scala.

The publishers would like to thank the following for supplying illustrations for this book:
Pages: 25 *tr* Janos, Middletons; 43 *tr* Roger Kent. Borders by Vanessa Card.

CONTENTS

4 WHAT IS A SAINT?

HOLY FAMILY
6 VIRGIN MARY
8 ST JOSEPH
9 ST ANNE
10 ST JOHN the BAPTIST

FOLLOWERS OF CHRIST
12 ST MARY MAGDALENE
14 ST PETER the APOSTLE
16 ST PAUL the APOSTLE
18 ST ANDREW
19 ST THOMAS

GOSPEL WRITERS
20 ST MATTHEW
21 ST MARK
22 ST LUKE
23 ST JOHN

MARTYRS
24 ST STEPHEN
26 ST SEBASTIAN
28 ST CATHERINE of ALEXANDRIA
29 ST AGNES
30 ST CHRISTOPHER
31 ST CECILIA
32 ST JOAN of ARC

GREAT THINKERS AND EVANGELISTS
34 ST AUGUSTINE
36 ST PATRICK
38 ST THOMAS AQUINAS
39 ST TERESA of AVILA

PEACE AND HEALING
40 ST FRANCIS of ASSISI
42 ST ELIZABETH of HUNGARY
43 ST ROSE of LIMA
44 ST NICHOLAS
45 ST BERNADETTE
46 BRITAIN'S FAMOUS SAINTS

ANGELS
48 WHAT ARE ANGELS?
50 GUARDIAN ANGELS
51 CHOIRS OF ANGELS

ARCHANGELS
52 ARCHANGEL MICHAEL
54 ARCHANGEL GABRIEL
56 ARCHANGEL RAPHAEL
58 FALLEN ANGELS

60 CALENDAR OF FEAST DAYS
62 GLOSSARY
64 INDEX

WHAT IS A SAINT?

detail from ST AMBROSE WITH DONORS AND ST LOUIS, ST PETER, ST PAUL AND ST SEBASTIAN
Bartolomeo Vivarini (1432–99)
Galleria dell'Accademia, Venice, Italy

FEAST DAY
1 November – known as All Saints' Day

The name 'saint' is given to a Christian person who has died and is worthy of great honour and respect. The name comes from the Latin word *sanctus*, meaning holy.

The first people to be made saints were Christ's family, his apostles and the early Christian martyrs in the first century. These people were very well known and became saints by word of mouth. The saints were given a feast day – a day of celebration that fell on the anniversary of their death rather than their birth. After all, death was the moment when the saints were taken into heaven.

With the passing centuries, however, it was less easy to decide who was and was not worthy of being a saint. Eventually, in 1170, the Pope decided that he should approve all new saints in a process called canonization. This is still how people become saints today.

detail from THE CRUCIFIXION WITH THE VIRGIN AND SAINTS
Fra Angelico (c. 1387–1455)
Museo di San Marco, Florence, Italy

THE VIRGIN MARY WITH THE APOSTLES AND OTHER SAINTS
Fra Angelico
(c. 1387–1455)
The National Gallery, London, UK

There are many thousands of saints from all walks of life – peasants, princesses, teachers, soldiers, writers, doctors. Some saints travelled and did good works; others started religious houses, and lived lives of simplicity and prayer. Most of them had a special gift – of loving God, of caring for the needy, of healing or teaching, of patience and wisdom. While some saints' lives are little more than legend, others are all too real. Many of the early saints faced persecution, torture and a brutal death.

For many Christians, the saints play an important role. They were once human, just like us, with human weaknesses and fears. Now that they are in heaven, close to God, they may act as valuable go-betweens, watching over us, protecting us, caring and praying for us. The saints in this book led extraordinary lives. Most of them faced enormous problems, and met death with courage and faith. As some of the world's most inspiring role models, they can show us how to live.

VIRGIN MARY

Mary is the most important of all the saints – a person so good and holy that she was chosen to be the mother of God's own son. Mary loved Jesus and, in spite of her trust in God, suffered greatly as she watched him die.

detail from
THE VIRGIN AT PRAYER
Sassoferrato (1609–85)
The National Gallery, London, UK

Mary lived in Nazareth, Galilee. She was a gentle young woman who was engaged to a carpenter called Joseph. One day, the archangel Gabriel visited her and told her that she would have a baby who would be the son of God. Mary was amazed, but obediently replied, 'I am God's servant and I will do as he asks.'

Months later, when the baby was due, Mary and Joseph travelled to Bethlehem to register for their taxes. The town was so busy that they had to stay in a stable, and this was where Jesus was born. Mary was overjoyed at her baby boy and, weeks later, she took him to the temple and dedicated him to God.

Mary loved Jesus with all her heart. As he grew up, she saw how special he was. She was with him when he performed his first miracle. They were both at a wedding in Cana when the wine ran out. Mary told Jesus about the problem and he changed jars of water into wine!

Mary knew that Jesus was doing God's work on earth. Still, she must have been very frightened when he was arrested and sentenced to death. She suffered with him as he died on the cross.

Mary knew about Jesus' ascension into heaven. Many Christians believe that she, too, was taken into heaven.

FEAST DAY
15 August – the day Mary is believed to have been taken up into heaven

PATRON SAINT
The entire human race

THE MADONNA OF HUMILITY
Lippo di Dalmasio (c.1352–1410/21)
The National Gallery, London, UK

St Joseph

Joseph was husband of Mary, mother of Jesus, and the protector of the Holy Family. Although he wasn't Jesus' birth father, he loved and taught the young boy as if he were his own son.

Joseph, a carpenter from Nazareth, was engaged to Mary. He was a simple, honest, respectable man. He must have been surprised when Mary told him she was expecting a baby, and amazed when an angel explained to him that the baby was the son of God!

Joseph felt responsible for the Holy Family and always did his best to protect them. He found the stable where Jesus was born. He hurried the family to safety in Egypt, after an angel warned him that King Herod was planning to murder all baby boys. Like any parent, Joseph did what he could to bring up Jesus properly.

It is thought that Joseph must have died while Jesus was still young. We learn nothing about Joseph in Jesus' adult life, and he was not there when Jesus was crucified.

THE HOLY FAMILY WITH THE LAMB
Raphael, originally Raffaello Sanzio (1483–1520)
Museo del Prado, Madrid, Spain

Joseph is often shown with a budding stick, a carpentry tool or a lily.

FEAST DAY
19 March

PATRON SAINT
Carpenters
The church
Fathers of families
Social justice
Working men

St Anne

The legend of St Anne tells how, after years of being childless, a holy woman had a daughter called Mary and became grandmother to the baby Jesus.

St Anne, the Virgin and the Baby
Ambrosius Benson
(c. 1495–1550)
Museo del Prado, Madrid, Spain

Feast day
26 July – shared with her husband St Joachim

Patron saint
Canada
Childless people
Grandmothers
Pregnant women

There are no historical facts known about Anne, the woman who is said to be the mother of Mary. But, in the early centuries of Christianity, a story grew up about her. She was said to be married to a man called Joachim, who lived in Nazareth. After twenty years of marriage, the couple had no children, which made them very unhappy. At last, Joachim decided to go into the desert for forty days and forty nights, and pray for a child. While he was away, Anne was visited by an angel, who told her that God had heard their prayers, and that they would have a child. Anne was so grateful when her daughter, Mary, was born, that she dedicated her to God.

Anne's legend tells us that she was a loving mother, who brought up Mary to put her trust and faith in God. When Mary herself gave birth to a child, Anne was devoted to her grandson, Jesus.

ST JOHN *the* BAPTIST

JOHN THE BAPTIST
Paolo Veronese, real name Paolo Caliari (1528–88)
Galleria Estense, Modena, Italy

FEAST DAY
24 June

PATRON SAINT
Baptism
Farriers
Motorways

John the Baptist was a prophet who prepared people for the coming of a great leader called the Messiah. As soon as John saw Jesus, he knew that he was God's chosen one – the Messiah.

John was the son of Zechariah and Elizabeth, a cousin of Mary. One day, while Zechariah was in the temple, he was visited by the archangel Gabriel, who told him that his wife would have a son who would become a great prophet – a messenger of God.

John grew into a remarkable man. To prepare for life as a prophet, he lived in the desert for many years, wearing a coarse hair shirt, and eating nothing but locusts and honey. John became a powerful preacher and huge crowds gathered to hear him. He told them to prepare for the arrival of the Messiah, a leader promised by God. He urged them to confess their sins, and be baptized in the River Jordan. One day, Jesus came to be baptized. John recognized him instantly – he was the Messiah!

John was fearless and outspoken, even of the rich and powerful. When King Herod Antipas married his brother's wife, Herodias, John protested and was sent to prison. Herodias hated John and wanted him dead. Her chance came when her daughter, Salome, danced for Herod and was offered a gift in return. Salome, acting on her mother's behalf, asked for John's head. Instantly, the order went out, and the prophet was beheaded.

THE BAPTISM OF CHRIST
Joachim Patinier (c. 1475/80–1524)
Kunsthistorisches Museum, Vienna, Austria

ST MARY MAGDALENE

Mary Magdalene was a devoted friend of Jesus and was with him when he died. Days later, her sorrow turned to joy, as she became the first person to see him risen from the dead.

MOLI ME TANGERE
Beato Angelico
(1387–1455)
Museo di San Marco,
Florence, Italy

Mary Magdalene lived in a small town by the Sea of Galilee. She suffered from a dreadful illness, caused by seven devils. One day, she was cured by Jesus when he visited her town. Immediately, she was baptized a Christian and she became his devoted follower. She was with Jesus at his crucifixion, and stayed with him and his mother until the moment he died.

Two days later, Mary and some other women went to the tomb to anoint Jesus' body with perfumes and spices. When they got there, they found the tomb empty and the huge stone that was blocking the entrance had been rolled away. Mary, heart-broken by the loss, sat weeping by the tomb.

Soon, a man came up to comfort her. She thought he was just the gardener, but when he gently spoke her name, she realized it was Jesus! He told her to go and tell the disciples that he had risen from the dead. With her heart full of joy, Mary ran to Jesus' friends to tell them the good news.

Nothing more is known about Mary. One legend says she sailed west to present-day France, where she became a preacher; another says she travelled east with St John and the Virgin Mary to the ancient Greek city of Ephesus, where she eventually died.

FEAST DAY
22 July

PATRON SAINT
Repentant sinners

THE MAGDALEN
about 1530, Netherlandish
The National Gallery, London, UK

St Peter *the* Apostle

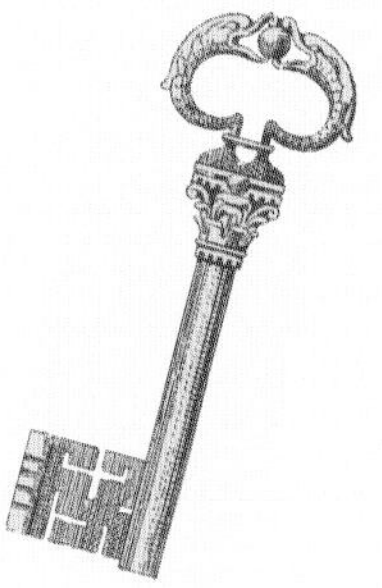

Jesus told Peter that he would be given the keys to the kingdom of heaven. Painters often show Peter with a set of keys.

Feast day
29 June

Patron saint
Fishermen
Rome

Peter was a fisherman who loved and followed Jesus. Peter is probably the best known of all the disciples, and became not only their leader but the leader of the Christian church.

Peter, who was first known as Simon, lived near the Sea of Galilee. One day, as he and his brother Andrew were fishing, Jesus passed by and asked them to follow him. Jesus gave Simon the name of Peter, which means rock, saying that he was the rock on which God's church would be built.

Peter was always at Jesus' side and he saw him perform many miracles. When Peter and the disciples were in a boat on the stormy waters of the Sea of Galilee, they saw Jesus walking across the water. Peter, a hasty, warm-hearted man, jumped out of the boat to meet his master and found that he, too, could walk on the water! But suddenly he panicked and began to sink before Jesus came to his aid.

Jesus loved Peter and saw a great strength in him, but sometimes the disciple let him down. One night, Peter denied ever knowing Jesus and deserted him after his arrest. But after the resurrection, Jesus forgave Peter and asked him to lead his church.

Peter travelled far and wide, telling all sorts of people about Jesus and, with God's help, performed miracles, too. Years later, he arrived in Rome. At this time, Christians were persecuted and, in about CE 64, Peter was arrested and crucified. His tomb is said to lie at St Peter's Basilica in the Vatican in Rome.

Saint Peter Preaching
Pedro Serra (14th century)
Fine Art Museum, Bilbao, Spain

ST PAUL *the* APOSTLE

After years spent persecuting Christians, Paul had a blinding vision and was converted to Christianity. He was one of the most important missionaries and founders of the Christian church.

FEAST DAY
29 June

PATRON SAINT
Missionaries
Tent-makers

Paul, who was first called Saul, was a Roman citizen who had been taught by the Greeks. He was also a Jew who followed his religion strictly. He had never met Jesus, and did not believe he was the Messiah. Saul hated the Christians and he had many of them arrested. He wanted to stamp out this new religion!

One day, when he was riding to the city of Damascus, Saul was blinded by a bright light. He heard the voice of Jesus ask, 'Saul, why are you persecuting me?' Saul was led into Damascus where, three days later, Jesus restored his sight. Saul realized that Jesus was truly the Messiah, and was baptized. From that day onwards, he was known as Paul.

Paul became a great preacher and writer, and an important missionary. He travelled tirelessly for many years, performing miracles and spreading the word of Jesus. He wrote letters to his new Christian groups, offering encouragement and advice.

Paul had many adventures and was often in trouble. He was beaten, imprisoned, stoned and shipwrecked, but he never lost his faith. Finally, he was arrested and sent to Rome. There, he is believed to have been beheaded with a sword and buried outside the city walls.

St Paul is often shown holding a book and a sword.

SAINT PAUL ON THE ROAD TO DAMASCUS
Lodovico Carracci (1555–1619)
Pinacoteca Nazionale, Bologna, Italy

SAINT PAUL
Tommaso Masaccio (1401–28)
Museo di San Matteo, Pisa, Italy

St Andrew

Feast Day
30 November

Patron Saint
Fishermen
Fishmongers
Greece
Russia
Scotland

Andrew was one of Jesus' twelve disciples and one of his close friends. Less well-known than his brother, Peter, Andrew followed Jesus all his life and, like him, he died on a cross.

Andrew was a fisherman, and a follower of John the Baptist. When John told people that Jesus was the Messiah, Andrew believed him and followed Jesus. One day, Jesus saw Andrew and his brother fishing, and asked them to become his disciples, saying, 'I will make you fishers of men.' Andrew answered Jesus' call, and urged his brother, Peter, to join him.

Andrew saw his master perform many miracles. One day, Jesus was preaching to a huge crowd of people who were very hungry. Andrew found a boy with two loaves and five fishes, and took the food to his master. Jesus miraculously used it to feed over 5,000 people!

Little is known about Andrew's later life. It is thought he became a missionary, and was crucified on an X-shaped cross. It is said that he preached for two whole days before he eventually died.

Saint Andrew
Carlo Crivelli (c. 1430/35–94)
The National Gallery, London, UK

St Thomas

The disciple Thomas found it so hard to believe that Jesus had risen from the dead that, nearly 2,000 years after his own death, he is still known as Doubting Thomas.

Feast day
3 July

Patron saint
Architects
Blindness
India
Pakistan

Thomas was one of Jesus' disciples. After Jesus rose from the dead, he appeared to his disciples – but Thomas was not there. Later, when Thomas heard the amazing news, he simply could not believe it! He declared, 'Unless I see in his hands the print of the nails and place my finger in their mark and place my hand in his side, I will not believe.'

Poor Thomas! He must have felt very ashamed when he saw Jesus one week later, and his master invited him to touch his wounds! Jesus gently forgave Thomas, but he said 'Blessed are they that have not seen, and yet have believed.'

Little more is known about Thomas. He is said to have been a missionary in India, and is believed to have been killed with a spear.

The Incredulity of Saint Thomas
Giovanni Battista Cima da Conegliano (c. 1459–1517)
The National Gallery, London, UK

St Matthew

Feast day
21 September

Patron saint
Accountants
Book-keepers
Tax collectors

Once hated as a tax collector, Matthew became one of Jesus' disciples. He is best known as the writer of the first book of the New Testament – the Gospel according to St Matthew.

Matthew, who lived in Galilee, was a tax collector. Tax collectors were hated and shunned by people, and banned from some temple services. The fact that the taxes went to the Romans made matters even worse! In spite of this, Jesus called on Matthew to become one of his most trusted friends.

Matthew gave up a well-paid job to spend all his time with Jesus. Years later, long after Jesus had died, Matthew wrote down everything he could remember about Jesus' life. His writings became the first of the four gospels.

No one knows exactly how Matthew's life ended. Legend tells us he preached in Ethiopia, where he died for his faith.

Saint Matthew the Evangelist
from a 12th century Byzantine evangelistary
Biblioteca Nazionale, Marciana, Venice, Italy

St Mark

Mark was a companion of the disciples Peter and Paul, and he worked alongside the early missionaries. He was a brilliant, intelligent man, and the author of the second gospel.

Mark is usually shown holding his gospel. His other special symbol is a winged lion.

FEAST DAY
25 April

PATRON SAINT
Venice

Mark lived in the city of Jerusalem. He was the son of a wealthy and important woman, who was one of the first Christians. Her house was a meeting place for the disciples, and Mark met them often. He soon became interested in what they had to say and was baptized a Christian.

Mark decided to become a missionary, travelling first with the disciple Paul and later with his cousin, Barnabas. When Mark eventually arrived in Rome, he became a close companion of Peter. Years later, when Mark came to write his gospel, he put in the stories that Peter had told him about the life and teachings of Jesus.

Mark's later life is shrouded in legend. It is said that he sailed to Egypt, but was captured and killed. About 700 years later, in CE 829, his remains were taken to Venice where, it is said, they still lie today inside the famous Basilica of St Mark.

MARK THE EVANGELIST
Michele di Matteo da Bologna (traceable 1416–47)
Galleria dell'Accademia, Venice, Italy

ST LUKE

Luke's symbol is an ox – the animal of sacrifice – because Luke's gospel begins with Zechariah's sacrifice in the temple.

A doctor, a historian and a fine writer, Luke was a man of many talents. He was the author of the simple but moving account of Jesus' birth that millions of us know today.

LUKE THE EVANGELIST
Agnolo Bronzino (1503–72)
Cappella Capponi, Santa Felicità, Florence, Italy

Luke was a Greek doctor who lived in Antioch. He was baptized by some of the first missionaries, several years after Jesus' death and resurrection.

Luke was a great friend of Paul, and travelled with him on two of his missionary journeys. When Paul was arrested and sent to Rome, Luke decided to go with him. During the voyage, their ship broke up in stormy seas. But, with God's help, Paul, Luke and every crew member managed to swim to shore.

Luke was a great writer with a gentle heart. The stories he told showed how Jesus cared for everyone – for women and men, non-Jews as well as Jews, and for people who were poor and sick.

Luke lived to a fine old age. As well as writing the third gospel, he wrote a history of the early Christian church, which he called the Acts of the Apostles. He is believed to have died peacefully in Boeotia, in ancient Greece.

FEAST DAY
18 October

PATRON SAINT
Artists
Craftsmen and women
Doctors
Surgeons

St John

Once a follower of John the Baptist, John left behind a content fisherman's life to become a disciple of Jesus. In later years, he wrote down everything he had seen in the Gospel according to St John.

FEAST DAY
27 October

PATRON SAINT
Bookbinders
Printers
Theologians
Writers

John and his older brother, James, were successful fishermen in Galilee. But when Jesus called them to become his disciples, they turned their backs on their work.

John spent a lot of time with Jesus and became one of his most devoted friends – so much so that, moments before he died, Jesus asked John to take care of his mother, Mary.

In later years, John suffered hardship and imprisonment as he helped to build the Christian church. After travelling in Turkey and Greece, he went to Rome, where the emperor had him thrown into boiling oil. Miraculously, John survived. In his last years, he returned to Turkey, where he worked on his gospel. John was over 90 when he died.

detail from MADONNA DELL 'UMILTA'
Giovanni da Bologna (14th century)
Galleria dell'Accademia, Venice, Italy

St Stephen

Stephen was the first Christian martyr – the first person ever to die for the Christian faith. He lived at a time when it was dangerous to be a Christian, and he was sentenced to a brutal death.

Stephen was a helper in the early Christian church. He was one of seven people chosen by the apostles to help them spread the message of Jesus and look after the poor. Stephen was a very special person. As well as being a devoted Christian, he was a wise and educated man. He gave inspiring talks and attracted many followers.

Stephen encouraged many people to become Christians. He explained that Jesus had died to save people from their sins, and had risen again to show his power over death. People who believed in Jesus would have eternal life.

Sadly, Stephen made powerful enemies among the Jewish elders. They did not believe that Jesus was the Messiah and they hated the new Christian church. Again and again, they argued with Stephen, but he patiently stood his ground. In the end, they made up charges against Stephen and took him to the Jewish court.

In the courtroom, Stephen criticized his accusers for not believing in Jesus. Looking up, he told them he could see a vision of Jesus with God in heaven. This so angered the court that it ordered Stephen to be stoned to death. In this cruel and violent way, he became the first Christian martyr.

Saint Stephen
Il Francia, (Francesco di Marco Raibolini) (1450–1517)
Galleria Borghese, Rome, Italy

Stephen is often shown with stones, the symbols of his martyrdom.

Dates
Died around CE 34–5

Feast day
26 December

Patron saint
Builders
Deacons

St Sebastian

Feast day
20 January

Patron saint
Archers
Athletes
Soldiers

Sebastian was a Roman soldier with a deadly secret – he was a Christian. He lived at a time when the emperor, Diocletian, was persecuting Christians. Sebastian risked his life inside the enemy camp to help his fellow believers.

Sebastian was a double-agent. While he appeared to be one of the emperor's loyal guards, secretly he was comforting Christian prisoners, and converting prison guards.

The emperor, who admired Sebastian, asked him to be one of his personal bodyguards. But when he discovered Sebastian's true faith, Diocletian was furious and ordered him to be shot with arrows. The execution was carried out and Sebastian was left for dead, but a woman called Irene found him still alive and nursed him back to health.

With great courage, Sebastian returned to the emperor, and protested against his cruelty. Diocletian ordered him to be clubbed to death. This time, Sebastian died of his wounds. A church now stands on the spot outside Rome where he is believed to be buried.

Saint Sebastian
Gerrit van Honthorst (1592–1656)
The National Gallery, London, UK

Saint Sebastian
Raphael, originally Raffaello Sanzio (1483–1520)
Accademia Carrara, Bergamo, Italy

ST CATHERINE *of* ALEXANDRIA

The spiked wheel, on which Catherine was to be tortured, appears in many paintings of the saint. It gave its name to the Catherine-wheel firework.

FEAST DAY
25 November

PATRON SAINT
Librarians
Preachers
Scholars
Young girls
Millers, spinners, potters and anyone who works with wheels

The story of Catherine is shrouded in legend. The story goes that this wealthy, educated and fearless young woman was angered by Roman persecution of the Christians and challenged the Emperor Maxentius himself!

detail from SAINT CATHERINE OF ALEXANDRIA AND SAINT DOMINIC
Carlo Crivelli (c. 1430/35–94)
The National Gallery, London, UK

Catherine lived in Alexandria – a city in Egypt under Roman rule. When Emperor Maxentius heard that she was speaking out about his treatment of the Christians, he sent fifty scholars to convert her back to pagan gods. But Catherine argued with the scholars and converted them to Christianity! A furious Maxentius tried to win Catherine over by asking her to marry him. She refused, saying that she was a 'bride of Christ'. Later, she was imprisoned and ordered to be tortured on a wheel of spikes. But the wheel broke, and so Maxentius had her beheaded instead. Catherine's faith was stronger than scholars, the promise of riches or the fear of death. Her body was taken to Mount Sinai, where her shrine still stands today.

St Agnes

The legend of St Agnes tells of a young girl who was so devoted to Christ, that she decided never to marry. Christians like Agnes faced persecution from the Romans and her decision cost Agnes her life.

Agnes is believed to have lived in Rome, Italy, in about 340–350. As the beautiful, young daughter of a wealthy family, many men wanted to marry her. However, Agnes refused them all, saying 'Christ is my bridegroom. He was the first to choose me. I shall be his alone.' One man who had hoped to marry Agnes was so angry at this refusal that he betrayed her to the Romans. Shortly after, Agnes was arrested and ordered to give up her Christian beliefs. She bravely and calmly stood by her faith, and chose to be executed instead. Roman writers of the time praised Agnes for the incredible courage she showed.

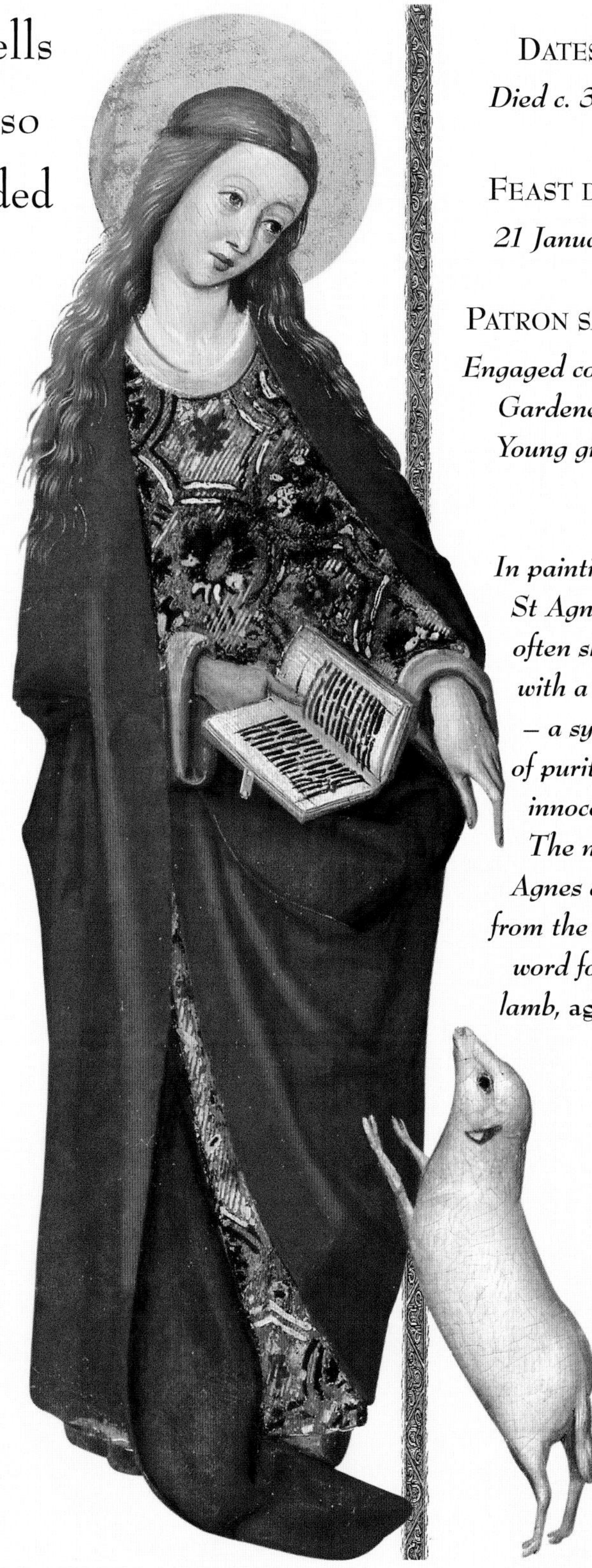

detail from THE CRUCIFIXION WITH SAINTS
Master of Liesbon (mid- to late-15th century)
The National Gallery, London, UK

DATES
Died c. 304

FEAST DAY
21 January

PATRON SAINT
Engaged couples
Gardeners
Young girls

In paintings, St Agnes is often shown with a lamb – a symbol of purity and innocence. The name Agnes comes from the Latin word for a lamb, agnus.

St Christopher

Feast day
25 July

Patron saint
Motorists
Sailors
Travellers

The legend of St Christopher is very well-known. It tells how a man of great strength struggled to carry a child across a river. This, of course, was no ordinary child – it was Jesus Christ.

Christopher was a huge man – in fact, he was more of a giant. He lived by a river and worked as a ferryman, carrying people across the water. Christopher had learned about Jesus Christ and dearly hoped to meet him.

One night, a little child asked Christopher to carry him over the water. As the giant waded into the river, the water grew deeper and the child grew so heavy that Christopher feared they would drown. When they reached the other side, the child told him he was Jesus Christ, who 'carried the weight of the whole world on his shoulders'.

Legend says that Christopher later travelled to Turkey to tell people about Jesus. There, he was imprisoned and treated very harshly. He was beaten, shot with arrows and finally beheaded.

St Christopher
Dieric Bouts the Elder (c. 1410/20–75)
Alte Pinakothek, Munich, Germany

St Cecilia

Cecilia was said to hear heavenly music whenever she prayed to God. For her, music brought strength and comfort. It helped her to live through dangerous times and face a cruel death.

DATES
2nd to 3rd centuries

FEAST DAY
22 November

PATRON SAINT
Composers
Music
Musicians
Organ-builders
Singers

The story of Cecilia, who was born in Rome, is little more than legend. At an early age, she devoted herself to God. When she was promised in marriage to a man called Valerian, she was very unhappy. She prayed to God, and was comforted by the sound of heavenly music.

Valerian was a good man. He understood why Cecilia did not want a husband, and he not only respected her wishes, but became a Christian too. At this time, Christians were executed daily by the Roman authorities. When Valerian and his brother Tiburtius were discovered burying these Christian martyrs, they were also executed.

Cecilia never tried to hide her faith. She preached openly and converted people to Christianity. In time, she was arrested and later beheaded. As the sword struck, Cecilia sang to God and comforted herself with music.

SAINT CECILIA WITH AN ANGEL
Orazio Gentileschi (1563–1640)
Galleria Nazionale dell'Umbria, Perugia, Italy

ST JOAN *of* ARC

At a time when France was at war with England, a young French girl answered God's call and led her country to victory. She followed her conscience in the face of death and, years later, was made a saint.

JOAN OF ARC – detail from the *c. 1505* manuscript 'La Vie des Femmes Celebres' (Life of Famous Women)
Antoine du Four
Musze Thomas Dobrze, Nantes, France

Joan of Arc, the youngest daughter of a poor farmer, grew up in a small French village, and never learned to read or write. In 1425, at the age of 13, she began to hear voices who, she said, were the voices of saints. They commanded her to drive out the English army from France – surely an impossible task for a young girl!

But Joan was determined to follow God's will. Although she suffered many setbacks, she impressed people with her devotion and courage. When she met Charles, the crown prince of France, he gave her a small army. In April 1429, at the age of 17, she led her troops to a famous victory against the English, and freed the city of Orleans.

Joan, inspired by her voices, won victory in five more battles. By chance, she was captured and sold to the English. They wanted to get rid of her and charged her with witchcraft. At her trial, Joan spoke bravely about her voices and her calling from God, but the English sent her to a terrible death. On 30 May 1431, Joan was burned at the stake in the market-place in Rouen, France, and her ashes were thrown into the River Seine. Joan was made a saint 500 years later.

DATES
1412–31

FEAST DAY
30 May

PATRON SAINT
France
Soldiers

JOAN OF ARC AT THE CORONATION OF KING CHARLES VII
Jean-Auguste Dominique Ingres (1780–1867)
Musée du Louvre, Paris, France

St Augustine

DATES
CE 354–430

SAINT AUGUSTINE
Nicoletto Semitecolo
(14th century)
Santa Maria dei Servi,
Venice, Italy

FEAST DAY
28 August

PATRON SAINT
Theologians

St Augustine is one of the most important figures of the Christian church. A man of genius, he is famous not for the things he did, but for the things he thought and wrote.

Augustine was born in North Africa to a Christian mother and a pagan father. He was brought up as a Christian but, as he grew older, he lost interest in leading a good life and put aside his Christian faith.

Augustine studied public speaking. When he was about 30, he went to Rome and taught there as a professor. Yet he felt something important was missing from his life. He met with priests and bishops, and became interested in Christianity again. He was converted quite suddenly in his garden one evening, after reading some words of St Paul.

Augustine returned to North Africa and set up a monastery there. For the rest of his life, as a monk, a priest and the Bishop of Hippo, he preached to people and cared for the poor – but most of all he wrote. He wrote about his sinful past, his search for God, and about the history and teachings of Christianity. These writings have inspired and helped Christians for many hundreds of years.

detail from SAINT AUGUSTINE AND THE CHILD ON THE SEASHORE
Pinturicchio (1454–1513)
Galleria Nazionale dell'Umbria, Perugia, Italy

St Patrick

St Patrick was a humble man who had great energy and enthusiasm. He spent twenty-five years converting the Irish people to Christianity, at a time when Ireland seemed pagan and wild. He is now the most popular Irish saint.

St Patrick and a king
miniature from a manuscript 'Golden Legend of Jacopo da Voragine' *(c. 1260)*
Huntington Library and Art Gallery, San Marino, CA, USA

Dates
c. 385–461

Feast day
17 March

Patron saint
Ireland

Patrick, first known as Patricius, was born in Roman Britain. His father was a Roman citizen, and his grandfather a Christian priest. The boy was only a teenager when his life took a dramatic turn. He was captured by pirates, taken to Ireland and sold as a slave. For six years, he worked for an Irish chief, looking after sheep and pigs. Lonely, unhappy and longing to escape, he prayed to God day and night.

Eventually, Patrick escaped from slavery and boarded a boat for France. There, he had many more adventures before finally returning home. Patrick now decided to train for the priesthood. Although he was not well educated, he was deeply caring and sincere. His early years – as an exile, a slave and a runaway – had taught him to trust God completely.

In 435, Patrick was made Bishop of Ireland. To outsiders, Ireland seemed like the edge of the world. It did not belong to the Roman empire and Christianity was hardly known. Patrick was a very successful missionary. He converted Irish chiefs, set up monasteries and organized the growing church. He died in around 461 and has since become the best loved of the Irish saints.

The miracle of St Patrick of Ireland
Giovanni Battista Tiepolo (1696–1770)
Museo Civico, Padua, Italy

St Thomas Aquinas

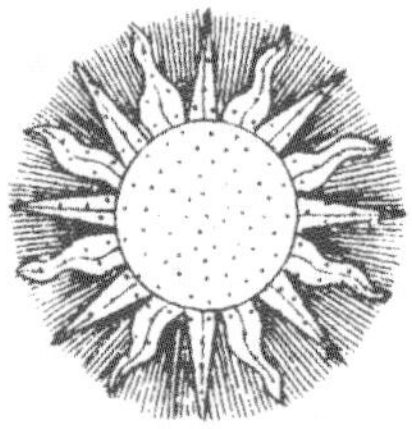

The sun is one of St Thomas's symbols, as well as a chalice and an ox.

DATES
1225–74

FEAST DAY
28 January

PATRON SAINT
Academics
Philosophers
Schools and colleges
Theologians

Thomas Aquinas was a large, silent man, nicknamed the 'dumb ox' by his fellow-students. Yet he proved to be one of the most important thinkers, writers and teachers the Christian church has ever known.

Thomas Aquinas was born into a wealthy Italian family and had a brilliant education. Yet, to the horror of his parents, he decided to become a monk.

As a monk, Thomas continued to study and his teachers were the best of the age. Soon, he was writing and lecturing at universities in Italy and France. Thomas's works are masterpieces of clear thinking and powerful argument – about the Bible, and Christian teachings and ideas. He wrote so much and worked so hard that he is said to have dictated his ideas to four different secretaries at a time!

Overwork led to Thomas's death at the early age of 49. Yet, 1,500 years later, his writings are still studied by theology students and would-be priests today.

ST THOMAS AQUINAS
Gentile da Fabriano (c. 1370–1427)
Pinacoteca di Brera, Milan, Italy

St Teresa *of* Avila

Teresa was a Spanish nun, who devoted her life to poverty and prayer. She set up convents all over Spain, and the books and letters she wrote for her nuns are still widely read today.

Teresa had many visions. In one, she is believed to have seen a dove. This has become one of her symbols.

Teresa was born in Avila, Spain, the daughter of noble parents. When she was a teenager, her mother died, and she decided to become a nun. The convent she joined was very easy-going, with frequent visitors from town. Teresa longed to live a simpler, more disciplined life. She spent many hours in deep prayer and began to have holy visions.

Teresa suffered years of ill health. When she recovered, she started a convent away from the distractions of the world. Here, Teresa and her nuns spent many hours alone with God in prayer. The rest of the time was spent on simple chores, such as sweeping and spinning. Though life was strict, Teresa was a warm, cheerful woman and greatly loved by her nuns. In time, she started sixteen more convents. She wrote letters of encouragement to them all, and her books about a life of prayer still make inspiring reading.

DATES
1515–82

FEAST DAY
15 October

PATRON SAINT
Lace-makers

TERESA OF AVILA'S VISION OF A DOVE
Peter Paul Rubens (1577–1640)
Fitzwilliam Museum, University of Cambridge, UK

ST FRANCIS *of* ASSISI

DATES
1181–1226

FEAST DAY
4 October

PATRON SAINT
Animals
Ecologists
Italy

St Francis gave up a life of wealth and comfort to help and care for the poor. He is a popular saint, particularly with children, and is fondly remembered for his love of animals and all of God's creation.

Francis lived in Assisi, Italy, and was the son of a wealthy merchant. He was expected to go into the family business, but he was more interested in helping the poor and sick. One day, he sold some of his father's goods and gave money to a ruined church. His father was so angry that Francis stripped off his rich clothes and turned his back on his family for ever.

His new life was one of poverty and prayer. He travelled from place to place, preaching and caring for the sick, and living on what people gave him. He devotedly nursed a man with leprosy – an illness greatly feared at the time – and publicly kissed the man's hand. Francis's strength and courage inspired people to follow him and, in time, he formed a group of monks known as the Franciscans.

Towards the end of his life, Francis had a vision of Christ on the Cross. When it was over, Francis found that his hands and feet were bleeding, just like the crucified Christ's. These wounds, known as stigmata, lasted until he died.

SAINT FRANCIS
Giovanni da Milano (1320–69)
Musée du Louvre, Paris, France

SAINT FRANCIS OF ASSISI GIVES CLOAK TO POOR HORSEMAN
Giotto di Bondone (1266–1337)
Upper Church of S. Francesco, Assisi, Italy

ST ELIZABETH *of* HUNGARY

Elizabeth was a royal princess, and her crown has become her symbol.

DATES
1207–31

FEAST DAY
17 November

PATRON SAINT
Bakers
Beggars
Charities
Lace-makers

For most of her short life, Elizabeth knew only wealth and happiness. When that happiness came to a sudden end, she turned her back on her comfortable life, and devoted herself to the poor.

Elizabeth was the daughter of the king of Hungary. When she was only four, she was engaged to a prince called Louis, and sent to live in Germany. Elizabeth grew up to love Louis. Years later, they married and had three children.

Elizabeth was a beautiful, compassionate woman, and very generous to the poor. Her life took a tragic turn when Louis suddenly died of the plague. Elizabeth was heart-broken. She was turned out of her home by Louis' brother and decided to join a Franciscan order.

She then lived a life of poverty, helping the poor and sick. She had a harsh spiritual teacher, who slapped her and beat her with sticks to keep her 'holy', but it only made her weak and ill. She died when she was only 24.

ST ELIZABETH OF HUNGARY SPINNING WOOL FOR THE POOR
Marianne Stokes (1855–1927)
Private Collection

ST ROSE *of* LIMA

St Rose was the first saint of the Americas. This beautiful young woman was not interested in marriage. Instead, she lived a life of holiness and hardship, and dedicated herself to God.

The rose is linked with St Rose's name and has become her symbol.

DATES
1586–1617

FEAST DAY
23 August

PATRON SAINT
Florists
Gardeners
Peru
South America

Rose was the daughter of a Spanish family, who lived in Lima, Peru. Unlike most women, she hated her beauty: she rubbed her face with pepper and cut off all her hair. Even though Rose had many admirers, she decided to become a nun. She lived in a hut in her garden at home, and spent many hours in prayer.

Rose believed that the more she suffered, the closer she could be to God. She wore a crown of roses and dug their thorns into her head. She wore a dress of the coarsest cloth. She fasted several times a week and would not drink to quench her thirst. Sadly, she became weak and, after a long illness, died when she was 31.

Rose is a popular saint. Huge crowds lined the streets at her funeral and her home has become a shrine.

detail from MARY WITH THE THREE HOLY DOMINICAN NUNS CATHERINE OF SIENA, ROSE OF LIMA AND AGNES OF MONTEPULCINO
Giovanni Battista Tiepolo (1696–1770)
S. Maria del Rosario, Venice, Italy

St Nicholas

Dates
4th century

Feast day
6 December

Patron saint
Children
Merchants
Russia
Sailors
Unmarried girls

Legend tells us that St Nicholas was a sweet, kind, generous man, who liked to help people in need. He is known around the world as 'Santa Claus' and is one of the most popular saints.

We know very little about St Nicholas. He was a bishop who lived in Myra, Turkey, at some time during the fourth century. There are many different stories about him. In one, he is said to have helped three young sisters, who were too poor to marry. Nicholas crept by their house one night, and threw three bags of gold through the window. This was a secret, generous act that asked for nothing in return. Stories about St Nicholas have spread from one country to another. It was the Dutch who first shortened his name to 'Claus' and called him Santa Claus. Today, he has become the secret visitor who leaves presents for good children. In some countries, children receive presents on his feast day; in others, on Christmas Eve.

detail from THE PERUGIA ALTARPIECE
Fra Angelico (c. 1387–1455)
Galleria Nazionale dell'Umbria, Perugia, Italy

St Bernadette

Bernadette was a poor girl from Lourdes, France, who had visions of the Virgin Mary. These have made her home town an important place of Christian pilgrimage.

Dates
1844–79

Feast day
16 April

Patron saint
Shepherdesses

Bernadette was only 14 when she had a vision of the Virgin Mary. Over the next six months, she had many more. In the visions, Mary spoke to Bernadette, led her to a spring of healing water and asked her to build a church.

Priests were suspicious of Bernadette's visions, and questioned her for many years. She stood by her story and was finally believed. A church was built on the site of her visions and it was said that the nearby spring was a place of healing.

Bernadette was quiet and humble, and did not enjoy the fuss. She entered a convent, where she worked and prayed. She had always suffered from asthma and ill health, and was only 35 when she died.

Bernadette Soubirous
French School (20th century)
Biblioteque des Arts Decoratifs, Paris, France

BRITAIN'S FAMOUS SAINTS

Britain is a country of four nations, each with its own patron saint: St George for England, St Patrick (see pages 36–37) for Ireland, St Andrew (see page 18) for Scotland and St David for Wales. The first British martyr was St Alban.

ST ALBAN'S FEAST DAY
22 June

St Alban (died c. CE 209)
Alban was a pagan soldier. One day, a Christian priest, who was being hunted by the Romans, asked to hide in his home. Alban was struck by the man's goodness and wisdom, and asked to be baptized. When soldiers arrived to arrest the priest, Alban put on the priest's clothes and was arrested in his place. He was beaten, tortured and condemned to death, but would not give up his faith.

As Alban was led to his execution, two miracles are said to have happened. First, a river parted to allow the group across. Then, a fountain sprang up out of the ground. The frightened executioner converted at these signs before beheading Alban.

ST DAVID'S FEAST DAY
1 March

St David (c. CE 520–601)
David was born in Wales. He was a monk and later a bishop in Pembrokeshire. He worked as a missionary, converting people and starting many monasteries. David's monks lived hard lives. They worked, studied and were not allowed to speak. David was a powerful preacher. Once, as David spoke to a crowd, it is said that a hill rose under his feet, allowing him to be seen.

Another story tells how before a battle David told Welsh soldiers to put a leek in their hats to avoid attacking one another. This is why leeks are associated with St David's Day.

St George (died c. CE 303)

St George's
FEAST DAY
23 April

George was not born in or ever visited England, but he was chosen as its patron saint because he was strong, courageous, willing to fight evil and to protect innocent lives.

George was born in the Middle East. Legend tells us that he saved a country that was being terrorized by a dragon. Every day, the beast demanded feeding – first with sheep, and later with humans. The next victim was to be the daughter of the king, but George came to her rescue. He attacked the dragon and tied it up, agreeing to kill it only if the people converted to Christianity. Everyone agreed, and 15,000 people were baptized on the spot!

Little is known about George's real life. He was probably a soldier in Emperor Diocletian's army. When the emperor began persecuting Christians, George may have complained. In the end, he was jailed, tortured and then beheaded.

What are angels?

Feast day
29 September – for all angels

Angels are God's messengers. In the Bible, these beautiful beings are sent from heaven to people on earth to deliver help, warnings or exciting news.

Angels are holy beings that were created by God and know the Creator face-to-face. The word angel comes from the Greek word *angelos*, which means messenger. Their appearances in the Bible are brief but important; they are a link between heaven and earth.

In the Bible, angels appear in different ways. Sometimes, they appear in a blaze of glory, dazzling onlookers and filling them with fear. This is how the angels appeared to the shepherds in Bethlehem on the night that Jesus was born: 'And, lo, the angel of the Lord came upon them, and the glory of the Lord shone round about them: and they were sore afraid.'

detail from Polyptych of the Dominicans, cusp: Announcing Angel
Fra Angelico (c. 1387–1455)
Galleria Nazionale dell'Umbria, Perugia, Italy

Angels sometimes appear to people while they are asleep. An angel appeared to Joseph in his dreams to tell him that Mary was expecting the son of God. At other times, angels take human form. In the Old Testament, Abraham meets three strangers, whom he invites into his tent for a meal. It is only when they tell him that his wife, Sarah, will have a child, that he realizes they are really angels.

BIRTH OF CHRIST
Robert Campin (Master of Flemalle)
(c. 1375/80–1444)
Musée des Beaux-Arts, Dijon, France

As well as delivering important messages, angels also provide practical help. At times, they protect those who show obedience to God: in the Old Testament, an angel protects Daniel when he is thrown into the lions' den. At other times, they protect those who do God's work: in the New Testament, an angel frees Peter from prison, by breaking his prison chains.

The Bible tells us that angels worship God alone. They are happy when people come to know and love God. Indeed, when humans die, angels are said to welcome them and carry them into heaven.

GUARDIAN ANGELS

ST PETER FREED FROM PRISON
Sebastiano Ricci (1658–1734)
Santa Stae, Venice, Italy

Some Christians believe that guardian angels exist to help and protect us. They suggest that, at the moment of our birth, each of us is given a guardian angel to accompany us through life. This comforting idea has existed for many thousands of years and is even mentioned in the Bible.

When Peter the apostle is thrown into prison by Herod Antipas, his fellow Christians pray for his safety. These prayers are heard by God, who sends an angel to the prison. The angel removes Peter's chains. At first, Peter thinks it is all a dream, but when the angel leads him to freedom, he realizes that the angel was sent by God to deliver him from Herod.

Some Christians believe that guardian angels are always present to help us – they are our partners on the pathway to heaven. People can call on the angels to protect them in their struggle to lead good lives.

Choirs of Angels

Countless angels are said to exist in heaven. This fact once so fascinated Christians that they attempted to sort these heavenly beings into different groups. Some groups of angels had specific roles, and were said to perform particular tasks.

The highest group are the archangels. Only three – Michael, Gabriel and Raphael – are named in the Bible, even though Raphael says he is one of seven. The archangels are mighty beings who are very close to God and have the power to bring about great change.

Two other groups of angels are the cherubim and seraphim. They are said to surround and worship the throne of heaven, and to serve God day and night. The Book of Genesis tells us that when Adam and Eve were banished from the Garden of Eden, God sent the cherubim to guard the Tree of Life.

There is an important difference between the archangels and the cherubim and seraphim. Archangels have contact with people on earth; cherubim and seraphim do not.

ANGELS
Benozzo Gozzoli
(1420–97)
Palazzo Medici-Riccardi,
Cappella dei Magi,
Florence, Italy

ARCHANGEL MICHAEL

Michael is God's most trusted creature and carries out heaven's commands. A fierce warrior, comforting guardian and protector against evil, Michael is the greatest angel of them all.

ARCHANGEL MICHAEL
(14th century)
Byzantine Museum, Athens, Greece

Michael is heaven's most powerful archangel. In the Old Testament, Daniel calls Michael 'one of the chief princes' and believes the angel to be the guardian of the Israelites. The very name, Michael, means 'who is like God' – a good name for an angel who acts with great authority, almost as a deputy for God.

Michael is a champion of right and justice, and fights evil at every turn. When one of God's angels, Lucifer, started a war in heaven (see pages 58–59), Michael fought and defeated the rebels and threw them out of heaven. No wonder Michael is known as the warrior angel and is often painted wearing full armour.

There are several legends about Michael. In one legend, it is said that the angel appeared in Rome at a time of dreadful plague. This may be why Michael is said to protect the sick and receive their souls into heaven.

Michael is also believed to be a guardian of high places. Two monasteries dedicated to Michael – St Michael's Mount in Britain and Mont St Michel in France – were both built on outcrops of rock.

FEAST DAY
29 September – known as 'St Michael and all the angels'

PATRON
Brussels
Police officers
The sick

THE ARCHANGEL MICHAEL
Pietro Perugina (1469–1523)
The National Gallery, London, UK

ARCHANGEL GABRIEL

The name Gabriel means 'the hero of God'.

FEAST DAY
29 September

PATRON SAINT
Broadcasters
Messengers
Postal workers
Telecommunication workers
Writers

The archangel Gabriel is the best-known of all the angels. It was Gabriel who appeared to Mary, and told her the exciting news that she was to have a baby, who would be the son of God.

Gabriel is mentioned several times in the Bible, and always as the bringer of important news. In the Old Testament, the angel appeared to Daniel in the form of a man. Gabriel helped Daniel to understand a puzzling vision and prophesied the coming of Jesus.

In the New Testament, Gabriel appeared to Zechariah, saying 'I am Gabriel who stands in the presence of God'. The angel told Zechariah that he would have a son called John, who would grow up to be a great prophet – the famous John the Baptist. Zechariah didn't believe this news and so God took away his power of speech until the baby was born. A few months later, God sends Gabriel to tell Mary about the birth of Jesus – the son of God.

Many artists have painted the scene where Gabriel tells Mary about the birth of Jesus. This is known as the Annunciation.

THE ANNUNCIATION
Zanobi Strozzi (c. 1395–1455)
The National Gallery, London, UK

THE ANNUNCIATION: THE ANGEL GABRIEL
Ferrari Gaudenzio (c. 1508–46)
The National Gallery, London, UK

Aue

Archangel Raphael

The name Raphael means 'God heals.' In a wonderful story, the caring archangel shows a young man called Tobias how to heal his father's blindness.

Angel
Raphael, originally Raffaello Sanzio (1483–1520)
Pinacota Civica T. Martinengo, Brescia, Italy

There is a story about Raphael and a man called Tobit, who lived long before Jesus was born. Tobit was a good man who helped the poor but, one night, he suddenly lost his sight. His blindness was a great burden to him, and he prayed to God to let him die. God heard his prayers and sent Raphael to help.

Meanwhile Tobit was preparing for death. He asked his son, Tobias, to collect some savings from a place called Media. Raphael appeared to Tobias in human form, explained that he was a distant relative and went with him on the journey.

One day, Tobias caught a fish. Raphael told him to remove its insides, which he said could be used as a cure. Weeks later, when the travellers returned home, Raphael told Tobias to rub the fish on his father's eyes. Miraculously, Tobit's blindness was cured!

Then Raphael revealed his true identity: 'I am Raphael, one of the seven holy angels who... enter in the presence of the glory of the Holy One.' The angel told Tobit and Tobias to praise and thank God, before vanishing and returning to heaven.

Feast day
29 September

Patron
The blind
Doctors
Nurses
Travellers

detail from The Virgin and Child with an angel, the archangel Michael, and the archangel Raphael with Tobias
Pietro Perugino (1469–1523)
The National Gallery, London, UK

FALLEN ANGELS

SATAN IS CHAINED FOR A THOUSAND YEARS
Juan Gerson (16th century)
Church of the Franciscan monastery, Tecamachalco, Mexico

The Bible mentions only four angels by name – Michael, Gabriel, Raphael and Lucifer. In the beginning, they were all created good, but one of them, Lucifer, was tempted into sin and became God's enemy.

There is a famous story about the angel, Lucifer. Lucifer, whose name means 'light bearer' was very, very proud. In time, the angel wanted to sit on the throne of heaven and enjoy the worship that belonged to God alone. Lucifer must have been very persuasive – soon one-third of all the angels agreed to join the rebel angel in the fight against God. This is how war broke out in heaven.

Small parts of this story appear in old translations of the Bible, in the Book of Revelation; others have been added by writers over the years. The story goes that the archangel Michael fought Lucifer and the rebel army and, acting on God's will, threw them out of heaven. At this point in the story, Lucifer was given a new name – Satan. The fallen archangel was chained up in a dark pit for a thousand years.

Satan tried to tempt people away from God in several Bible stories. When Jesus went into the wilderness for forty days and nights, Satan encouraged him to challenge God and use his power for his own ends. Later, Satan tempted Jesus' disciple, Judas, to betray his master for 30 pieces of silver. Satan is also known by other names, such as Beelzebub and the Prince of Darkness.

THE THREE ARCHANGELS
Marco d'Oggiano (c. 1470–1530)
Pinacoteca di Brera, Milan, Italy

CALENDAR OF FEAST DAYS

** indicates the saints featured in this book*

JANUARY

2 St Basil the Great
12 St Benedict
14 St Sava
17 St Anthony Abbot
19 St Henry of Uppsalla
20 *St Sebastian
21 *St Agnes
24 St Francis de Sales
28 *St Thomas Aquinas
31 St John Bosco

FEBRUARY

1 St Brigid
3 St Anskar
8 St Jerome Emilian
9 St Apollonia
14 St Cyril
St Methodius
St Valentine
19 St Boniface
23 St Polycarp

MARCH

1 *St David of Wales
2 St Chad
17 *St Patrick
19 *St Joseph
20 St Cuthbert
24 St Iranaeus, Bishop of Sirmium

APRIL

4 St Isidore
11 St Stanislaus
16 *St Bernadette
17 St Stephen Harding
23 *St George
St Adalbert of Prague
25 *St Mark
29 St Catherine of Siena
30 St Pius V

MAY

19 St Dunstan
27 St Augustine, Archbishop of Canterbury
30 *St Joan of Arc

JUNE

2 St Erasmus (Elmo)
5 St Boniface
9 St Columba
11 St Barnabus
13 St Anthony of Padua
22 St Alban
24 *St John the Baptist
28 St Irenaeus, Bishop of Lyons
29 *St Paul
*St Peter

JULY

3 *St Thomas
11 St Benedict
15 St Bonaventure
20 St Margaret of Antioch
22 *St Mary Magdalene
23 St Bridget of Sweden
25 *St Christopher
St James the Great

26 *St Anne
St Joachim
29 St Olaf
31 St Ignatius of Loyola

August

8 St Dominic
10 St Lawrence
11 St Clare
14 St Maximilian Kolbe

15 *Virgin Mary
16 St Stephen of Hungary
20 St Bernard
21 St Pius X
23 *St Rose of Lima
24 St Bartholomew
26 St Ninian

28 *St Augustine, Bishop of Hippo

September

1 St Giles
3 St Gregory the Great
9 St Peter Claver
13 St John Chrysostom
17 St Hildegard
21 *St Matthew
28 St Wenceslaus
29 All angels
30 St Jerome

October

1 St Térèse of Lisieux
4 *St Francis of Assisi
6 St Bruno
9 St Denis
10 St Francis Borgia
13 St Edward the Confessor
15 *St Teresa of Avila
16 St Gall
18 *St Luke
19 St Isaac Jogues
25 St Crispin
27 *St John the Apostle

28 St Jude
St Simon

November

1 All Saints' Day
7 St Willibrord
11 St Martin of Tours
15 St Albert the Great
16 St Margaret of Scotland
17 *St Elizabeth of Hungary
22 *St Cecilia
23 St Clement I
25 *St Catherine of Alexandria
30 *St Andrew

December

1 St Edmund Campion
3 St Francis Xavier

4 St Barbara
6 *St Nicholas
7 St Ambrose
10 St Gregory III
13 St Lucy
19 St Anastasius I
26 *St Stephen
29 St Thomas à Becket

Glossary

anoint	to pour oil over someone or something to make it holy
apostle	one who is sent with the authority of Jesus, such as the twelve disciples, and St Paul
ascension	Jesus' return to heaven after he had been raised from the dead
baptize	to use water as a sign of faith, repentance and sin washed away, admitting the believer to the Christian church
crucifixion	a form of execution in which a person is fastened to a wooden cross
disciple	anyone who follows and learns from another, such as one of the twelve close followers of Jesus
eternal	something that is everlasting, without beginning or end
exile	the banishment of someone from their own country
Gospel	one of the first four books of the New Testament, which narrate Jesus' life
heaven	the place where God and his angels live, and where Christian believers will join God after death
martyr	someone who is ready to suffer and die for his or her faith
miracles	dramatic and surprising events that cannot be explained
missionaries	people who are sent to teach others about their religion
pagan	a person with no religious beliefs or who worships different gods
persecution	the unfair and cruel treatment of people because of their religion
pilgrimage	a journey to a shrine or other holy place
plague	an infectious disease that spreads quickly and kills many people
prophet	someone who receives messages from God and tells other people about them
resurrection	Jesus' return from death to a new life that would last forever
shrine	a place that is especially holy – for example, the tomb of a saint
theology	the study of religious ideas
visions	revelations from God that show events that have not yet happened

Notable people

Abraham	The man chosen by God to be the father of the Israelites. The Israelites were a great nation and God's chosen people, from whom the Jews were descended.
Barnabas	A friend and fellow missionary of St Paul and St Mark.
Daniel	An exiled Jew who worked in the royal court of Babylon. He was thrown into a lions' den because of his religion, but an angel was sent to protect him.
Diocletian	Roman emperor (CE 284–305) who ordered the persecution of the Christians.
Elizabeth	The wife of Zechariah and mother of John the Baptist.
Herod (the Great)	The king of Judea when Jesus was born, who ordered all the baby boys to be killed.
Herod Antipas	One of the sons of Herod the Great. He persecuted many Christians and ordered the beheading of John the Baptist.
Herodias	The wife of Herod Antipas, she wanted the head of John the Baptist.
Joachim	The husband of Anne, mother of Mary.
Judas	One of Jesus' twelve disciples. Judas betrayed Jesus to the Romans, leading to Jesus' arrest and death.
Maxentius	Roman emperor (CE 306–312) who ordered the persecution of the Christians.
Salome	The daughter of Herodias. Her dance for Herod Antipas led to the death of John the Baptist.
Sarah	The wife of Abraham.
Tobias	The father of Tobit, who became blind and was cured by the archangel Raphael.
Tobit	The son of Tobias, who was accompanied on a journey by the archangel Raphael, and helped to cure his father's blindness.
Zechariah	The father of John the Baptist.

INDEX

Abraham 49, 63
Acts of the Apostles 22
Agnes, St 29
Alban, St 46
Andrew, St 14, 18, 46
angels 7, 8, 48–49, 50, 51, 58–59
Anne, St 9
Annunciation 54
apostles 4, 13, 14–20, 21, 23
archangels 7, 10, 51, 52–57, 58–59
Augustine, St 34–35

Barnabas 21, 63
Bernadette, St 45
Bible 48, 49, 50, 51, 54, 58
New Testament 20, 49
Old Testament 49, 53, 54

canonization 4
Catherine of Alexandria, St 28
Cecilia, St 31
cherubim 51
Christopher, St 30
convents 39, 45

Daniel 49, 53, 54, 63
David, St 46–47
Diocletian, Emperor 26, 47, 63
disciples, *see* apostles
Doubting Thomas, *see* Thomas, St

Elizabeth 10, 63
Elizabeth of Hungary, St 42

Francis of Assisi, St 40–41
Franciscans 40, 42

Gabriel, archangel 7, 10, 51, 54–55, 58
George, St 46, 47
God 5, 7, 9, 37, 48, 50, 51, 57
Gospels
of St John 23
of St Luke 22
of St Mark 21
of St Matthew 20
guardian angels 50

heaven 4, 5, 6, 7, 48, 50, 51, 53, 58, 63
Herod, King 8, 63
Herod Antipas, King 10, 50, 63
Herodias 10, 63
Holy Family 4, 6–11

Jesus Christ 7, 8, 9, 10, 11, 13, 14, 17, 18, 19, 20, 23, 24, 30, 48, 54, 58
Joachim 9, 63
Joan of Arc, St 32–33
John, St 13, 23
John the Baptist, St 10–11, 18, 23, 54
Joseph, St 7, 8, 49
Judas 58, 63

Lucifer 53, 58
Luke, St 22

Mark, St 21
martyrs 4, 24–33, 46
Mary, Virgin 6–7, 8, 9, 13, 23, 45, 54
Mary Magdalene, St 12–13
Matthew, St 20
Maxentius, Emperor 28, 63
Messiah 10, 17, 18
Michael, archangel 51, 52–53, 58
miracles 7, 14, 18, 46, 57, 62
missionaries 17, 18, 19, 21, 22, 37, 46, 62
monasteries 5, 37, 46, 53
monks 38, 40, 46

Nicholas, St 44
nuns 39, 43

Patrick, St 36–37, 46
Paul, St 16–17, 21, 22, 34
Peter, St 14–15, 18, 21, 49, 50
Pope 4

Raphael, archangel 51, 56–57, 58
Romans 17, 20, 26, 28, 29, 31, 37, 46
Rose of Lima, St 43

Salome 10, 63
Sarah 49, 63
Satan 58
Sebastian, St 26–27
seraphim 51
Stephen, St 24–25
stigmata 40

Teresa of Avila, St 39
Thomas, St 19
Thomas Aquinas, St 38
Tobias 57, 63
Tobit 57, 63

Virgin Mary, *see* Mary, Virgin
visions 17, 25, 39, 40, 45, 63

Zechariah 10, 54, 62